CREEPY CRAWLIES

ALVIN SILVERSTEIN · VIRGINIA SILVERSTEIN · LAURA SILVERSTEIN NUNN

TWENTY-FIRST CENTURY BOOKS
BROOKFIELD, CONNECTICUT

Cover photograph courtesy of © Tom McHugh/Photo Researchers, Inc.

Photographs courtesy of Bruce Coleman, Inc.: pp. 6 (© Robert Carr), 26 (© Jean Claude Carton), 30 (© Alan Blank); Animals Animals: pp. 10 (© Richard Kolar), 22 (© Zig Leszczynski), 42 (© Brian P. Kenney); Visuals Unlimited, Inc.: pp. 14 (© Glenn M. Oliver), 38 (© Kjell B. Sandved); Photo Researchers, Inc.: pp. 18 (© Scott Camazine), 34 (© Andrew J. Martinez)

Library of Congress Cataloging-in-Publication Data

Silverstein, Alvin.
Creepy crawlies / by Alvin & Virginia Silverstein & Laura
Silverstein Nunn.
p. cm. — (What a pet!)
Summary: Describes insects, spiders, and other non-mammals most commonly
owned as pets, and offers advice on their care, feeding, and breeding.
Includes bibliographical references (p.   ).
ISBN 0-7613-2511-5 (lib. bdg.)
1. Insects as pets—Juvenile literature. 2. Invertebrates as pets
—Juvenile literature.   [1. Insects as pets. 2. Invertebrates aspets. 3. Pets.]
I. Silverstein, Virginia B. II. Nunn, Laura Silverstein. III. Title.
IV. Series: Silverstein, Alvin. What a pet!
SF459.I5S56 2003
639'.7—dc21
2002154601

Published by Twenty-First Century Books
A Division of The Millbrook Press, Inc.
2 Old New Milford Road
Brookfield, CT 06804
www.millbrookpress.com

CONTENTS

WHAT A PET!

THIS SERIES WILL GIVE you information about some well-known animals and some unusual ones. It will help you to select a pet suitable for your family and for where you live. It will also tell you about animals that should not be pets. It is important for you to understand that many people who work with animals are strongly opposed to keeping *any* wild creature as a pet.

People tend to want to keep exotic animals. But they forget that often it is illegal to have them as pets, or that they require a great deal of special care and will never really become good pets. A current fad of owning an exotic animal may quickly pass, and the animals suffer. Their owners may abandon them in an effort to return them to the wild, even though the animals can no longer survive there. Or they may languish in small cages without proper food and exercise.

Before selecting any animal as a pet, it is a good idea to learn as much as you can about it. This series will help you, and your local veterinarian and the ASPCA are good sources of information. You should also find out if it is a member of an endangered species. Phone numbers for each state wildlife agency can be found on the Internet at

www.rzu2u.com/states.htm

Any pet is a big responsibility—*your* responsibility. The most important thing to keep in mind when selecting a pet is the welfare of the animal.

FAST FACTS

Scientific name	Family Formicidae (ants), Order Hymenoptera
Cost	Around $10 depending on the type of ant farm (may include ants); or free if you make the ant farm yourself and collect your own ants
Food	Place a few drops of sugar water in the jar each day. (Tiny pieces of fruit, bread crumbs, or bits of meat may be added occasionally to see how the ants handle them. They should not be given regularly because they may get moldy.) Also include a damp sponge for drinking water.
Housing	An ant farm can be store-bought or made at home. Find a jar (gallon- or quart-sized). Put a block of wood in the center of the jar. Pour sandy soil or Perlite (sold in garden shops) into the jar around the object. The jar lid should have tiny holes in it, not large enough for the ants to squeeze through. Keep the ant farm in a darkened place. (It is dark in the ants' natural underground home.) Spray lightly with a water bottle as needed to keep the ant farm slightly moist.
Training	Ants, like other insects, do everything by instinct. They cannot be taught behaviors.
Special Notes	It is illegal to sell queen ants in the United States.

ANTS

WE DON'T LIKE IT when ants creep across the kitchen floor, and they always seem to be a nuisance at picnics. So why would people want to keep ants as pets? Because they are easy to care for and fascinating to watch.

Ants live in a very structured society, where everybody has important jobs to do. Keeping an ant farm can give you a close-up look into the ant world. Watching ants can be an amazing learning experience. Just don't let them escape from the ant farm!

> ### What Are Insects?
>
> *Ants are insects. There are at least 10,000 different kinds of ants and more than a million species of insects—more than all other kinds of animals combined. Although insects can vary greatly, they all have the same type of body. All insects have six legs and three body parts: a head, a thorax, and an abdomen. Many insects also have wings. Insects don't have bones. They have an outer covering, or exoskeleton, that protects them from harm. This exoskeleton is jointed like a knight's suit of armor, and this allows the insect to move.*

AN ANT'S LIFE

Ants are social insects. They live in very large groups, called colonies. A single colony may consist of hundreds, thousands, or even millions of ants! Ant colonies often live in a raised mound on the ground (an anthill), which contains a complicated maze of chambers (rooms) and connecting tunnels that may extend for yards underground. Entrances to ant colonies may also be found in the cracks of sidewalks or under rocks. Some ants dig their tunnels and chambers inside fallen trees and logs. The chambers include bedrooms and meeting places for large numbers of ants, storerooms for food, and nurseries for raising baby ants.

An ant colony includes three types of ants: the queen, the males, and the workers. Each ant in a colony has a special job to ensure the survival of their community, and to carry it out, they must work together as a team. The queen is the largest ant in the colony. Her job is to lay eggs. She can produce thousands of baby ants during her lifetime—and that can be up to twenty years or more! The workers make up most of the ant colony. They are all female, but they cannot lay eggs. Worker ants do most of the routine work. Some of them gather food, some dig tunnels, some are soldiers that fight to defend the colony, and some feed the queen and take care of the young ants. The males have just one purpose: to mate with the queen. Soon after the male's job is done, he dies. Males and young queens have wings, but a queen loses her wings after she mates with a male and settles down to lay eggs.

An ant colony is a very busy community. Much of the activity surrounds the queen. The queen stays warm and cozy in one of the chambers. She depends on the workers to feed her. Once the queen lays her eggs, workers take them to another chamber, the egg nursery. The workers care for the eggs and protect them from enemies, such as spiders. Like many insects, ants go through various life stages, in a process called metamorphosis. First, the eggs hatch into a pale, wormlike form, called a larva. Workers carry the larvae to another large nursery chamber, where they feed them and lick them clean. Soon each larva goes into a new stage of life. Inside its exoskeleton, the young ant, now called a pupa, begins to change. Its wormlike body seems to melt, and completely different body parts form. After two or three weeks, a fully formed ant breaks out of its exoskeleton.

Ants have very poor eyesight, but they can get along quite well by using the two long antennae attached to the top of the head. By tapping and probing a crumb with her antennae, an ant gets an idea of its shape and size, then picks it up and carries it back to the ant nest. The ant can pick up some pretty heavy objects—even several times heavier than her own body. But sometimes, when pieces of food are too big for one little ant to carry, she has to get some help. Hurrying back to the nest, the ant stops from time to time to touch the tip of her abdomen to the ground. Each time, she releases a tiny drop of chemical. Back at the nest, the ant is met by others from the colony. After sniffing at her with their antennae, some of the ants rush outside, sniffing at the ground. Soon they pick up the traces of scent the returning ant had laid down. Before long, a line of ants moves out from the nest, following the odor trail to the food.

ANT PETS

Ants can vary greatly in size; some are less than $\frac{1}{16}$ inch (2 mm) long, while others may be as long as an inch (25 mm). They may be black, brown, reddish, or yellowish. But black ants are the ones you're most likely to see.

If you want to keep your very own ant colony to take care of and observe, you can buy an ant farm through the mail, along with a supply of worker ants. You can also make an ant farm yourself and collect ants in your neighborhood. Make sure you take an adult on your ant-collecting adventure. These insects can bite or sting.

Where would you look to find ants? Remember, they are often found between the cracks of a sidewalk or under rocks. You may even see little anthills in yards. It's not a good idea to collect ants in fallen trees or rotting logs, where carpenter ants and termites live. Both carpenter ants and termites feed on wood, so you wouldn't want them running around loose in your home.

When searching for ants, take along a jar with tiny holes in the lid and a small paintbrush to sweep the ants into the container. If you find an anthill, dig into the ground with a shovel until you've reached the ants' nest. To have a strong colony, you should try to find the queen. You can recognize her because she's much bigger than the other ants. Her abdomen may be full of eggs. It's also important to collect at least fifteen workers. If you can find only worker ants, that's okay. You should get about thirty of them. Even without a queen, they are fascinating to watch. They can take care of themselves and will live for a few months. An ant colony complete with a queen, males, and many workers can keep you engaged for a much longer time.

> **DID YOU KNOW?**
> Ants and termites look very similar. But there's one important difference: Ants have a narrow "waist" behind the thorax and termites do not.

INTERNET RESOURCES

www.antcam.com "AntCam"

www.antcolony.org "Ant Colony"

www.myrmecology.org "Myrmecology"

www.surfnetkids.com/ants.htm "Surfing the Net with Kids: Ants—The BEST ant sites for kids, teachers, families"

FAST FACTS

Scientific name	Family Arctiidae (tiger moths), Order Lepidoptera
Cost	Free: Caterpillars can be caught around your home.
Food	Plantain, dandelion leaves, and other ground-level plants. Also include a damp sponge for drinking water. Old, withered food should be replaced with new fresh leaves. Leaves will last longer if the stems are wrapped in wet paper towels.
Housing	Caterpillars need a glass or plastic container at least 12 by 7 inches (30 by 18 cm). Put an inch of damp soil on the bottom. Spray lightly with water to keep soil damp, but not wet. Do not keep the caterpillar home in direct sunlight. Include materials for climbing, such as twigs, sticks, or small wood blocks. Wooly bears hibernate during the winter and will need dead leaves on the soil and a large, flat piece of bark to hide under.
Training	Caterpillars, like other insects, do everything by instinct. They cannot be taught behaviors.
Special notes	Only moths and butterflies that are caught in your area should be set free there. If you buy larvae, pupae, or live butterflies, check on local regulations before releasing them.

CATERPILLARS

HAVE YOU EVER WATCHED an inchworm creep along a twig? It stretches forward, holds on tight with its front legs, and loops the rest of its body into an upside-down U. Then it pushes forward to move along. If you move the inchworm to your finger, it will slowly creep up your arm. But it doesn't seem creepy at all. It kind of tickles.

Inchworms aren't really worms. They are a kind of caterpillar. Caterpillars are larvae that turn into moths or butterflies. An inchworm grows up to be a geometer moth. (Its name comes from the fact that it seems to be measuring the Earth as it creeps along.)

Keeping a caterpillar as a pet is a unique experience. You get to watch it go through metamorphosis, magically changing from a "creepy crawly" to a delicate creature that flutters through the air on wings.

> ### Butterfly or Moth?
> *Butterflies and moths both belong to the group of insects called Lepidoptera. The name, meaning "scaly winged," comes from the fact that their wings are covered in scales. How can you tell if it's a moth or a butterfly? Most butterflies are brightly colored and active during the day; moths are usually drab-looking and active at dawn or dusk. But there are some butterflies with dull-colored wings and some brightly colored moths that fly around in the daytime. Their antennae are the best clue: Butterflies' antennae have a small round knob at the tip; moths have feathery antennae.*

A STAGE OF LIFE

A butterfly or moth goes through four stages of life. It starts out as an egg, which develops into a caterpillar, or larva. The caterpillar has a long, wormlike body, with three pairs of legs and some tiny "protolegs" that cling to leaves and twigs like Velcro. A caterpillar is like a little eating machine, gobbling up plant leaves to store energy for its big change. As the caterpillar grows, its body becomes too fat for its exoskeleton, which cannot stretch or grow. So it must molt, or shed its outer covering, in order to become larger. Underneath is a new soft layer, which quickly hardens after the caterpillar wriggles out of its old exoskeleton. A caterpillar molts several times until it is fully grown.

Butterflies and moths lay huge numbers of eggs, and the hungry caterpillars can do a lot of damage to plants, trees, and crops. Gypsy moth caterpillars, for example, can kill a tree by stripping it of all its leaves. But birds and other predators help to keep them under control.

Many caterpillars have special defenses. Some are covered with bad-tasting poisonous chemicals that will make a predator very ill or even kill it. These caterpillars are usually brightly colored, with easy-to-recognize markings that are like warning signs. Animals quickly learn that species with such patterns are not good to eat. Some caterpillars are covered with sharp, prickly hairs that inject poisonous chemicals into the skin—an unpleasant experience for any animal, including you. Others have markings like big fake eyespots that may scare a predator away. Some caterpillars survive by blending into their surroundings. A green caterpillar crawling on a green leaf or stem is likely to be overlooked. Adult butterflies and moths may also use warning signs or camouflage as a way to survive.

Most caterpillars do not make it to their full size. The lucky ones attach themselves to a twig or branch or burrow underground, and form a pupa. Some moth pupae are covered with a silk cocoon that the larva has spun around itself for protection. A butterfly pupa, called a chrysalis, is often green or multicolored and is not covered with a cocoon.

Inside the pupa's exoskeleton, everything is changing. The caterpillar's body turns into a soupy liquid, and then starts developing into an adult. When it is time to emerge, the insect will molt once again and push its way out into the world. It spreads its wings to dry and is soon a beautiful butterfly or a moth. While the caterpillar larva had munching mouthparts, most butterflies and moths have a special strawlike mouth that is used for sucking nectar from flowers.

CATERPILLAR PETS

The best time to look for caterpillars is during spring and early summer. You can find them munching on plants or bushes around your home, walking along sidewalks, or crossing roads. Use a paintbrush to sweep the caterpillar into a jar, and cover it with a lid containing airholes. If you spot a caterpillar eating, break off the leaf it is feeding on and put it inside the jar. Don't try to pick up the caterpillar with your fingers, because some caterpillars have chemicals or prickly spines that can irritate your skin.

Some caterpillars are very picky eaters and will eat only a certain kind of leaf. So make a note of the plant your caterpillar was eating and collect some leaves as a food supply.

There are lots of different caterpillars that would make interesting pets. A popular one in the United States is the wooly bear caterpillar. This is the larva of a tiger moth. It is covered with stiff hairs all over its body, which may feel prickly to the touch. They can irritate your skin if you are not careful. Besides its prickly coat, the wooly bear is easy to recognize. One common species has a black band on both the front and rear parts of the caterpillar's body. The middle part is reddish brown.

You can make the caterpillar's home fun and interesting by including things it can climb, such as twigs, sticks, or a hanging string. In nature, caterpillars climb up and over all kinds of things. Wooly bears are fast movers, compared to other caterpillars. They can walk 4 feet (1.2 meters) in a minute.

DID YOU KNOW?
A wooly bear will curl up in a tight ball to protect itself when it is bothered or frightened. Its prickly hairs stick out in every direction. This defense is a lot like that of a hedgehog.

Caterpillars will start to change to a pupa during the summer, so have some twigs, sticks, soil, and bark available. Metamorphosis can take weeks or even months.

Watching a pupa day after day may not be very exciting. But it is well worth the wait to watch a brand-new moth or butterfly emerge. When the time comes, the outer case cracks and the adult insect crawls out. Inside the pupa, the wings were damp and tightly folded; now they spread out and stiffen as blood fills the veins. Soon the insect is ready to take its first flight. Moths and butterflies should be set free; if not, they will damage their wings by banging them against the walls of a container.

INTERNET RESOURCES

www.ex.ac.uk/bugclub/cater.html "Rearing Caterpillars"
www.melanys.tripod.com/caterpillars.htm "Kids and Caterpillars"
www.teacherwebshelf.com/classroompets/insectsandco-butterflies.htm "Classroom Animals and Pets—Insects and company—Butterflies"
www.tulane.edu/~ldyer/lsacat/index.htm "WWW.CATERPILLARS.ORG."

FAST FACTS

Scientific name	Family Gryllidae (crickets), Order Orthoptera
Cost	Crickets can be caught free around your home or can be bought at a bait or pet shop for about ten cents each.
Food	Dry dog food plus a water-soaked cotton ball or sponge for drinking water. Special cricket food for breeding crickets is available but expensive.
Housing	Crickets need a container at least 12 by 7 inches (30 by 18 cm). Put an inch of damp soil on the bottom. Spray lightly with water to keep soil damp, but not wet. Do not keep the cricket's home in direct sunlight. Include materials such as twigs and sticks; also toilet-paper roll, egg-carton container, or other items they can hide under.
Training	Crickets, like other insects, do everything by instinct. They cannot be taught behaviors.
Special Notes	Crickets should live in a warm environment, where the temperature is always above 65°F (18°C).

CRICKETS

EVERYBODY KNOWS ABOUT BIRD songs, but did you know that crickets make their own music? On summer evenings in the country, you can hear crickets *chirp-chirp-chirping*. Just like birds, crickets use their "songs" to communicate with other members of their species.

Crickets make really fun pets. Not only are these insects talented singers, they are quick jumpers and can put on an interesting show.

THE SOUND OF CRICKETS

Have you ever heard a chorus of crickets singing in your backyard? It sounds like all the crickets in the neighborhood are joining in this nighttime concert. Actually, though, only adult male crickets can sing. They have special songs to attract mates, to stake out their territory against other males, and to warn of approaching danger. Most crickets sing at night, although some, such as the field cricket, can also be heard during the day.

Crickets do not make sounds from their throat, as we do. They use their wings to chirp. Adult crickets have two pairs of wings, which usually lie flat on their backs, one pair on top of the other. Some crickets use their wings for flying; others never even get off the ground.

Like playing a violin, a cricket makes sounds by rubbing the sharp edge of one of his upper wings against a long bumpy vein on the side of the other. Back and forth, the cricket rubs one wing against the other, sending out *chirp, chirp, chirp* sounds.

When an adult male cricket plays music to get the attention of a potential mate, the female must decide if she likes what she hears. But a cricket doesn't have ears on its head, as you do. Its "ears" are actually on its front legs, just below the joints. They are tiny holes, covered with a membrane that vibrates like the top of a drum. Both males and females can hear.

If a female doesn't like a male's serenade, she may kick him in the face! (Crickets have very strong hind legs.) But when a male's song pleases her, the female strokes his antennae with hers. He begins to chirp softly, and then they mate.

One way you can tell whether a cricket is male or female is by the long, needlelike tube, called the ovipositor, that sticks out from the back end of the female's abdomen. A female cricket lays her eggs, one at a time, using her ovipositor to punch a hole in the ground or in the bark of a tree. She can lay hundreds of eggs during the mating season.

Crickets have a simpler life cycle than ants, butterflies, and moths. They go through what scientists call incomplete metamorphosis. When the egg hatches, a tiny version of an adult cricket emerges. There is no larval stage. The young cricket, called a nymph, does not yet have wings, just stubs. It is also lighter colored than the adults. Like other insects, a cricket has a tough exoskeleton and must molt in order to grow. It will molt five to fourteen times until it becomes adult-size and grows wings.

Adult crickets usually die in the fall. In some species, only the young nymphs make it through the winter; in others, the eggs survive and do not hatch until spring.

CRICKET PETS

There are a number of different kinds of crickets, but the field cricket is the most familiar one. It may be brown or black and may grow up to an inch (25 mm) long. It can be found in fields, pastures, lawns, roadsides, and woods, and may even sneak into your house.

Catching a cricket is not as easy as collecting a slow-moving caterpillar. Crickets can jump up to twenty or thirty times their body length! They are really quick to hop away when they feel threatened. So catching one may turn out to be quite an adventure. On your journey, take along a collecting jar. You may be able to find a cricket in its usual hiding places, such as under rocks, logs, or a pile of leaves. It helps if the cricket is chirping. You can try following the chirping sound, but don't be surprised if the cricket suddenly stops chirping when you've gotten too close. If you do spot a cricket, take the jar and quickly put it upside down over the cricket. Wiggle your hand under the jar and flip it right-side up. Then put the lid on. If this doesn't work, you can also try catching the cricket using cupped hands, and then putting it into the jar. But this can be quite a challenge.

If you can't find any crickets outside or you have trouble catching them, you can buy some at a bait shop or pet store, which often sell them as food for other animals.

To some people, cricket songs sound pleasant; others find the sound of chirping crickets annoying. If you want to have a cricket as a pet but don't like the chirping sound it makes, you're better off with a female.

Let's Get Ready to Rumble!

If you put two male Asian crickets together with no place to go, watch out! These crickets are much more aggressive than the species that live in the United States, and they defend their territories fiercely. If one ignores the warning chirps of a male who has claimed a territory, a furious fight breaks out. One cricket may whip the other with his antennae. Then they butt heads or close in for some serious wrestling. The "homeowner" hops on the intruder, and they roll around, grabbing each other with their front legs and biting with their jaws. If one cricket manages to flip the other over, the defeated fighter leaves.

These crickets can sure put on an action-packed show. That's probably why cricket fighting became a popular sport in China, as early as A.D. 960. In fact, Chinese royalty sponsored tournaments featuring cricket fights. Fighters were divided into heavy-, middle-, and lightweight categories. Bets were placed on fighters, and the champions were worth a lot of money.

Cricket matches are still a popular sport in China today. Video cameras zoom in close and display the fight on TV sets for the viewing audience.

INTERNET RESOURCES

www.insecta-inspecta.com/crickets/field/ "Field Crickets"

www.ex.ac.uk/bugclub/cricket.html "Cricket Caresheet"

www.earthlife.net/insects/cricket.html "The Care of Crickets"

www.pca.state.mn.us/kids/c-september.html "Crickets: September Creature of the Month—Minnesota Pollution Control Agency"

F A S T   F A C T S

Scientific name	*Lumbricus terrestris* in Family Lumbricidae, Phylum Annelida (segmented worms)
Cost	Free: Earthworms can be caught around your home.
Food	Soil, dead leaves; leafy vegetables (lettuce, celery leaves) should be washed first.
Housing	Any glass or clear plastic container. Should include alternating layers of soil, dead leaves, and sand. Put worms on top and let them tunnel down into the soil. Lightly spray the soil to keep it damp, but not wet. Keep the worms' home in a cool, dark place.
Training	Worms do everything by instinct. They cannot be taught behaviors.

EARTHWORMS

DOES TOUCHING A WORM give you the creeps? Lots of people get a little grossed out by a worm's slimy, squirmy body. And yet, worms are very important for keeping us humans alive! If you dig up some soil, chances are you will find a worm or two. These worms provide the soil with many important nutrients that plants need to grow. Without worms, we wouldn't have many of the foods we eat every day.

Did you ever wonder what worms do in their underground homes? You can find out by keeping a few as pets.

UNDERGROUND WIGGLERS

If you look closely at an earthworm, you will notice that its tubelike body is made up of a series of rings, or segments. Most earthworms have more than one hundred segments. A typical garden earthworm is about 3 or 4 inches (7 to 10 cm) long, but the biggest earthworms in the world can grow to more than 10 feet (3 m)! These giant earthworms live in Australian rain forests.

DID YOU KNOW?
There are many different kinds of worms. Some are harmful and live in the bodies of living organisms. Some live freely in the ocean. Those that live in the soil are known as earthworms.

Earthworms like to live in dark, damp soil, where they can tunnel easily. If the surface of the soil gets too cold, too hot, or too dry, they will tunnel down into the earth, as much as 3 feet (1 m) deep. In fact, worms generally stay underground all day, coming out only at night to feed on fallen leaves or to mate. An earthworm breathes through its skin, taking in oxygen dissolved in the moisture. It will die if its skin dries out. A layer of sticky mucus produced all over the worm's skin helps to keep it moist. (That is what makes the worm look and feel so slimy.) The mucus also helps the worm's slippery body slide through the soil.

An earthworm can literally eat its way through the soil. It takes in mouthfuls of dirt, which pass slowly through its long body. On the way, bits of food—rotting leaves, fungi, algae, and bacteria—are digested. The leftovers eventually pass out of a hole near the end of the worm's body in the form of long, worm-shaped wastes, called casts. Worm casts look like little clumps of mud, but they are actually rich in nutrients from the partly digested plant matter. These nutrients, in turn, fertilize the soil and help plants and other organisms grow. Worms also help gardens by loosening up the soil when they burrow. Their tunnels bring oxygen down into the soil and also help to drain water.

An earthworm does not have legs; it uses the strong muscles in its body to wriggle through the soil. These muscles can stretch the worm out so that it is very long and thin, squish it so that it becomes short and fat, or even make one part of the worm's body thin while another part is fat. Tiny bristles attached to many of the segments grab the tunnel walls and help to keep the worm from slipping.

Heads or Tails?

How can you tell which end of a worm is the head and which is the tail? An earthworm wriggles through the soil with the pointy end first. This pointy part is the mouth area. The broad, smooth band around the worm's body, called the clitellum, is closer to the head.

Have you ever seen lots of worms scattered along sidewalks and roads after a rainfall? When the ground is wet, they can move around more easily on the surface without the danger of drying out. This is the perfect time for them to look for mates, too.

Interestingly, each earthworm has both male and female parts, but every worm still needs a partner to mate. The two worms mate lying head to tail with each other so that the male part of one worm is lined up with the female part of the other. Each worm provides sperm that fertilizes the other worm's eggs. Eggs and sperm are deposited in a jellylike ring that forms around each worm's clitellum. As the worm wriggles along, the ring slides off and closes into an egg case that will protect the fertilized eggs. The eggs may take up to five months to hatch. Out of as many as twenty eggs in an egg case, only one or two will hatch. The other ones will become food for those that survived. When an egg is ready to hatch, a tiny version of an adult worm emerges.

WORM PETS

If you find a worm in your garden, don't try to pull it out of its burrow. It will probably grab hold of the ground with its tiny bristles, and you may break off a few segments. Instead, use your hands to dig underneath the worm and scoop it out. Then put it into a collecting jar. (Make sure you wash your hands after touching worms.)

Fill a glass or clear plastic container with alternating layers of soil, sand, and dead leaves, and then place the earthworms on top. Water the soil every two or three days to keep it moist but not soggy. In a few days you will see some of the earthworms' tunnels through the soil. Keep the jar in the dark most of the time. Otherwise, the worms will make all their tunnels in the inner part of the soil, where you can't see them. Place some fresh leaves on top of the soil about once a week, and watch when and how the worms feed.

Nature's Cleanup Crew

Earthworms break down the remains of dead plants and animals, as well as waste materials, releasing nutrients into the soil. Without such decomposers, rotting logs, fallen leaves, and dead animals would pile up all over.

Worm decomposers in a compost heap turn organic waste into fertilized soil. You can make a compost pile outside or in a bucket with holes in the top, sides, or bottom. Fill the container with damp, shredded newspaper, vegetable peelings, eggshells, coffee grinds, grass clippings, leaves, and a little soil. Then add worms. You need red wigglers, which are sold in pet stores or bait shops. (The earthworms in a garden can't feed on kitchen wastes.) Sprinkle water on the compost to keep it moist (but not wet). Don't put too much garbage in the compost bin, or it may start to smell. When the compost is done, it can be used in gardens or as mulch for plants. Don't release the red wigglers in the garden, though. They can't survive there.

INTERNET RESOURCES

www.nysite.com/nature/fauna/earthworm.htm "The City Naturalist—Earthworms"

www.ag.usask.ca/cofa/departments/hort/hortinfo/yards/earthwor.html "Earthworms: Friend or Foe?"

www.cityfarmer.org/wormcomp61.html "Composting with Red Wiggler Worms"

yucky.kids.discovery.com/noflash/worm "Worm World"

FAST FACTS

Scientific name	*Coenobita clypeatus* (purple claw crab) in Family Coenobitidae
Cost	About $5 in pet shops or gift shops at coastal beaches
Food	Commercial hermit crab food. Treats include fresh fruits, such as apples, bananas, pears, and grapes, and vegetables, such as romaine lettuce (not iceberg), cabbage, carrots, and broccoli. They will also eat grains, such as crackers and cereals. Include a shallow water dish to avoid drowning. Water should be filtered because it may contain too much iron, which is harmful to hermit crabs.
Housing	At least a 10-gallon (38-liter) tank for one hermit crab, a larger size when keeping multiple hermit crabs. Keep a tight mesh covering over the tank since hermit crabs are well-known escape artists. Put a few inches of sand on the bottom of the tank. (Hermit crabs like to burrow in the sand, especially during molting.) Include rocks and sticks for climbing, and a good selection of shells. Shells can be bought at a pet store. Mist your crabs and their home with lukewarm water to keep the humidity level up. (Hermit crabs are more active when they are moist.)
Training	Hermit crabs that are handled often will become tame and enjoy being around people.
Special Notes	Temperatures should remain warm, in the range of 70° to 85°F (21° to 29°C).

HERMIT CRABS

HOW WOULD YOU LIKE A PET that carries its home on its back? No, it's not a turtle; it's a hermit crab. Hermit crabs, like turtles, depend on their hard outer shell to protect themselves from danger. But hermit crabs don't really own their own shells—they borrow them. They live in empty snail shells. When a hermit crab gets too big for its shell, it looks for a new one.

You can watch a pet hermit crab crawl around, climb up on things, bury itself in the sand, and try on new shells. If cared for properly, this pet can give you years of enjoyment.

LIVING IN A BORROWED HOME

Hermit crabs are usually found along the coastal shores in tropical regions, such as the Florida Keys, the Caribbean, and Venezuela. Most of them live in the sea, but the ones that are kept as pets are adapted to live on land. Land hermit crabs have gills, which must stay moist for them to breathe. If the gills dry out in the hot tropical sun, the crab will die. Hermit crabs store an extra supply of water in their shell. Still, they need to spend their days where it is cool, hiding in shallow burrows or underneath rocks, leaves, and fallen branches. They can't live underwater, though; their gills are much smaller than those of marine hermit crabs, and they would drown.

The hermit crab carries around a borrowed "house" along with it wherever it goes. Its body is shaped somewhat like a banana, and can twist into an empty snail shell for a perfect fit. Just like any other shell-wearing creature, this crab uses its shell for protection against predators. When a predator gets too close, the crab pulls its body into its shell and hides inside.

The hermit crab's body is made up of two main parts: the cephalothorax (a combination of head and thorax), and the abdomen. The head contains a mouth, two sets of antennae, and eyes on the ends of two long stalks. Attached to the thorax are five pairs of legs. Two pairs are walking legs. Another two pairs are used for holding onto

DID YOU KNOW?
Most kinds of crabs move sideways along the seashore, but hermit crabs walk forward.

23

the shell. The pair of legs in front are the crab's powerful claws. One claw is much larger than the other; it is used to block the shell's entrance, like an armored door, if the crab wants to sleep or hide from an enemy. The crab uses its smaller claw to tear apart food and carry bits of it to its mouth.

A tough exoskeleton covers the hermit crab's body. This outer covering is thicker in some places, such as the claws and back, acting like a suit of armor. But in other parts, such as the legs and joints, the exoskeleton is paper thin and can break off easily if pulled too hard.

The hermit crab must shed its exoskeleton in order to grow. When it is ready to molt, the crab looks for a safe hideaway, such as down in the sand, under leaves, or in a burrow. The old exoskeleton cracks open down the back, and the crab wriggles out of it. Underneath is the new exoskeleton, which is soft and moist. The crab is very vulnerable at this time and hides until the exoskeleton hardens. Stored water helps to keep it from drying out.

Hermit crabs molt throughout their lives. Young crabs molt several times a year, but an adult crab may molt only once every twelve to eighteen months.

Now that the hermit crab is larger, it may find that its old shell is too tight. So it has to start looking for a bigger one. When a hermit crab finds an empty snail shell, it inspects it carefully, rolling the shell over and running its claws over the inside and outside. It may try the shell on for size. If the crab doesn't like the way it feels, it will return to its old home and continue its search. But if the shell fits, the crab will abandon the old outgrown shell and slip backward into its new home. It may eat the old shell, which contains calcium and other important nutrients that help to strengthen the new exoskeleton.

HERMIT CRAB PETS

Hermit crabs have been popular pets for years. You can buy them in many pet stores or gift shops along coastal boardwalks. The purple claw crab is the kind most commonly sold. Hermit crabs can vary greatly in size, measuring from an inch (3 cm) to more than 6 inches (15 cm) long.

Despite their name, hermit crabs do not like to live alone. In fact, in the wild they are often found in large groups, crawling over one another and resting together in huge piles. It's a good idea to buy two or more hermit crabs so they won't get lonely. It's also a lot more fun watching several crabs interact with each other. Keep hermit crabs that are close in size. Larger hermit crabs have been known to eat smaller ones.

Hermit crabs are not aggressive, but, if necessary, they will fight each other for shells. This is not very common among land hermit crabs in the wild, but it may happen in captivity if they are not given enough shells to choose from. By tapping each other with their legs and claws, one crab will try to force the other away from the desired shell. Sometimes a crab will try to fight for a shell that is already occupied. It uses its legs and claws to rock the shell back and forth, occasionally jabbing the crab inside the shell. Eventually, the victim is forced out of its shell, and the attacker moves in.

Picking a hermit crab up for the first time may be painful. If you're not careful, it will clamp its claw onto your finger and hold on. The crab will let go if you put it under running lukewarm water. When you handle a hermit crab, pick it up on the top or back of the shell and keep your hand flat (as it sits on your palm) to avoid getting pinched. Make sure there is a surface close by so it won't get hurt if it falls. Crabs that are handled often will not be so frightened and are less likely to hurt you.

If you notice that your hermit crab is not eating, is not very active, and stays in one place, don't worry. It is probably getting ready to molt. Molting can take up to a month. Be patient and provide some new shells for your pet to choose for its new, bigger self.

Land hermit crabs will not reproduce in captivity. Females have to release their eggs in the ocean. After the babies are born, they start their lives on land.

INTERNET RESOURCES

www.thefunplace.com/house/pets/hermit.html "Hermit Crabs"

www.animalnetwork.com/critters/profiles/hermitcrab "Critter Collection: Hermit Crab"

www.klsnet.com/crab.html "Hermit Crabs"

www.geocities.com/Heartland/Hills/9459 "The Happy Hermit"

FAST FACTS

Scientific name	*Coccinella novemnotata* (nine-spotted ladybug) and *Coccinella septempunctata* (seven-spotted ladybug) in Family Coccinellidae, in Order Coleoptera (beetles)
Cost	Free: Ladybugs can be caught in or around your home. A thousand ladybugs can be purchased from garden supply stores for about $13 (plus shipping).
Food	Raisins, soaked in water. Include a water-soaked paper towel or cotton ball for drinking. (Ladybugs can drown in a water dish.)
Housing	A 4-by-7-inch (10-by-18-cm) container covered with a mesh top. Include a few small plants or leaves and twigs for climbing. Lightly spray water into the container every few days.
Training	Ladybugs do everything by instinct. They cannot be taught behaviors.
Special Notes	Ladybugs like light and warmth. Keep them in an area that receives a lot of sunlight, but not in direct sunlight. If you buy ladybugs by mail, make sure they are the right kind for your local area before releasing them.

LADYBUGS

WHAT KINDS OF INSECTS spend a lot of time on plants, but don't eat them? That would have to be ladybugs, because ladybugs are meat-eaters! These cute little spotted creatures feed mostly on plant-eating aphids, very tiny insects that can do a lot of damage to food crops.

Who can resist these adorable insects, crawling around in their colorful, spotted coats? Keeping ladybugs can be a lot of fun, especially since these little critters will readily walk onto your finger and up your arm. (Fortunately, they won't bite or sting you.)

What's in a Name?

Ladybugs aren't really bugs. People tend to call all insects bugs, but true bugs belong to a particular group. Ladybugs are actually beetles and are sometimes called ladybird beetles.

Not all ladybugs are ladies. In fact, many of the ones you see are probably males. The name ladybug *dates back to the Middle Ages when these spotted insects were called "Beetle of Our Lady," in honor of the Virgin Mary. People believed that these insects were gifts from heaven, sent to save the crops. Even today, some people consider ladybugs as a sign of good luck, good weather, and plentiful crops.*

COLORFUL CRAWLIES

Ladybugs are best known for their bright red coat covered with black spots. But they actually come in different colors and patterns—red, a blend of red and orange, or completely orange. Some ladybugs may even be black with red or yellow spots. The number of spots also varies from one (or even none) to more than twenty. Different kinds of ladybugs are often named for their spots. Some common ones are the seven-spotted ladybug and the nine-spotted ladybug. There are more than 4,000 different kinds of ladybugs found in many parts of the world.

Just like many other insects, ladybugs go through various stages of life as they grow to be adults. The life cycle starts when a female ladybug lays her eggs, which she usually attaches to leaves with a sticky "glue." She produces hundreds of eggs, but she deposits them in batches in different places. That way, if a predator eats one batch of eggs, the others will still have a chance to survive.

After about a week, the eggs hatch, and out come alligator-shaped larvae with six tiny legs. The larvae are black with orange or white markings on their long abdomens. They have tremendous appetites and will feed on anything they can— aphids, scale insects, and even each other! As the larvae eat and eat, they grow very quickly. Soon they become too fat for their exoskeletons, and they must molt. As they grow, the larvae have to molt three to four times until they are ready to change into a pupa. The pupa is orange and black and is usually attached to leaves, stems, or rocks. The pupal stage generally takes five to six days.

Easy Prey

Aphids are soft-bodied insects that attach themselves to a leaf and suck the plant juices. A mother aphid gives birth to live babies. As soon as she produces one, it attaches to the leaf right behind her and starts to feed on its own. Then the mother aphid moves forward a bit, sinks her snout into the leaf, and sucks more plant juice. As she continues to produce babies, there is soon a whole string of aphids along the leaf. So even a crawling ladybug larva can just go along and scoop up one after another. A ladybug uses its jaws to bite into its prey; its legs are good only for walking.

Aphids don't have any real defenses, but some of them have bodyguards. Aphids make a special sugar-water mixture that ants love, called honeydew. Some ants take care of the aphids so they can have a constant supply of this sweet juice. If a ladybug tries to eat their aphids, the ants come to the rescue and attack the ladybug.

When the adult ladybugs finally emerge, they have typical insect parts: six legs, antennae, and three main body parts. Attached to the thorax are two sets of wings, an inner pair used for flying and an outer pair called the elytra. The elytra are soft, wet, and yellow-colored at first. As they dry, they darken and become hard like a shell, helping to protect the ladybug's soft body. It takes up to twelve hours for the spots to appear. (Have you ever seen a ladybug fly? The elytra lift up, and the wings underneath flutter rapidly.)

Ladybugs can be found in large groups looking for aphids on plants in gardens or around farmer's crops. Aphids can do enormous damage to food crops, but ladybugs are welcome guests. They help farmers by getting rid of these destructive pests. A single ladybug may eat more than fifty aphids a day, and a ladybug larva may eat about twenty-five aphids a day. Many people are starting to use ladybugs to protect their crops instead of pesticides, which are harmful not only to insect pests, but to ladybugs as well.

LADYBUG PETS

How many flying insects do you know that would let you catch them? Very few—and ladybugs are one of them. You can find ladybugs crawling on plant leaves in flower gardens, vegetable gardens, or on weeds and shrubs. They may even live in people's houses, crawling around the windows. Usually you'll see clusters of ladybugs together. These cute little critters don't seem desperate to get away, so they're pretty easy to catch. Carry along a collecting jar and use a small paintbrush to sweep the ladybugs into the jar. Or you may put your finger in front of the ladybug and let it crawl on you. Then you can sweep it into the jar.

Ladybugs should be kept in a small container, about 4 by 7 inches (10 by 18 cm), so that they can find their food easily. You can keep several ladybugs in a single jar so they are more interesting to watch. But don't keep too many, because they eat a lot; make sure they get enough to eat. Ladybugs are picky eaters. In the wild they eat only live food, such as aphids or scale insects, which could become pests if they get loose in your house, infesting houseplants and pets. Fortunately, pet ladybugs can live on a diet of raisins soaked in water, although they won't breed without the chemicals they normally get from aphids.

Enjoy your ladybug pets. Take them out for a walk on your hand, but be very careful with them.

INTERNET RESOURCES

www.discoverlearning.com/webjourneys/ladybugs/ "Discover Learning Web
  Journey—LadyBugs"

www.enchantedlearning.com/subjects/insects/Ladybug.shtml "Ladybugs—
  Enchanted Learning Software"

www.entro.vt.edu/Fruitflies/lady.html "Lady Beetles"

www.geocities.com/Athens/Atrium/5924/schoolyardscience.htm "Ladybug
  Thematic Unit"

FAST FACTS

Scientific name	*Oxidus gracilis* (garden millipede); *Archispirostreptus gigas* (giant millipede) in Order Diplopoda (millipedes)
Cost	Common 1-inch (2.5-cm) millipedes can be caught free around your home; giant tropical millipedes cost about $12.
Food	Rotting plants, fruits (apples, bananas), and vegetables (lettuce, cucumbers)
Housing	A 5- or 10-gallon (19- or 38-liter) tank with a tight-fitting mesh lid. (Millipedes are good climbers and can use their strong heads to push their way out if the lid isn't tight.) Put 4 to 6 inches (10 to 13 cm) of sphagnum moss (not peat moss) from a garden center in the container. Put food in a wide-mouth jar that the millipede can crawl into and out of comfortably; place the jar in the moss. Lightly spray water into the container every day. Keep millipedes away from direct sunlight.
Training	Millipedes do everything by instinct. They cannot be taught behaviors.
Special Notes	Tropical millipedes may be illegal to own in some areas. Check your local regulations.

MILLIPEDES

MILLIPEDES HAVE LOTS OF LEGS—more than any other creepy crawly. In fact, the word *millipede* means "thousand feet," although millipedes don't really have a thousand legs. Most adult millipedes have 200 to 300 legs. That's still a lot!

Millipedes aren't as creepy as they look. If you catch one and let it crawl on your hand, it won't bite you. You may just feel a little tickle as it slowly crawls along your skin.

Going with the Flow

Have you ever tripped over your own two feet? A millipede has hundreds of legs, but it isn't clumsy at all. When it walks, each pair of legs moves together, but the pairs of legs on the other segments move at a slightly different time. So the legs flow in a wavelike motion. This helps to keep the legs from bumping into one another.

A MILLIPEDE'S LIFE

A millipede has a wormlike body that is made up of many segments. Unlike a worm with its soft body, though, a millipede is covered by a hard exoskeleton. Two pairs of walking legs are attached to most of the segments. The legs are fairly short, so a millipede walks very slowly. Millipedes can range greatly in size, from less than 1/8 inch to as much as 11 inches (1 mm to about 4 cm) long! Millipedes live in many places all over the world, but the giant ones can be found in tropical regions.

Millipedes hide out during the day in dark, damp places, such as moist soil, underneath rocks and logs, or under a pile of leaves. They use their strong little legs and hard, helmetlike heads to push their way through soil or under bark. When millipedes tunnel down into the soil, they gobble up dirt and plant material. They also eat fallen leaves, wood, and rotting plants, fruit, and dead animals. Like earthworms, millipedes are great decomposers, breaking down organic waste and eventually turning it into fertilized soil. They are also scavengers, clearing away the bodies of dead animals and plants and turning their nutrients into forms that other plants and animals can use.

Millipedes move very slowly, so they can't run away from their enemies. But they do have some defenses. A millipede might curl up into a tight ball like a hedgehog, with its head protected in the middle. Its exoskeleton protects it from most predators. Many millipedes will give off a very smelly odor if they are bothered. Not only do they smell bad, they taste bad too. An animal that tries to eat a millipede will get a bad taste in its mouth, and will probably remember not to bite these creatures in the future.

Chemical Weapons

Different kinds of millipedes make different chemicals to use against their enemies. Some produce camphor, the chemical that people use in mothballs and other insect repellents. Others produce a substance that makes attackers fall asleep when they eat it. While this may not save the victim, it can help its neighbors. Still other millipedes produce tiny amounts of poison gases. These help to keep away small predators, such as fire ants. Some tropical millipedes can spray smelly chemicals at larger animals, such as birds, mammals, or lizards, up to 5 feet (1.5 m) away!

Despite their defenses, many millipedes end up getting eaten by spiders, toads, and other predators. But don't worry—a single female millipede can lay as many as 300 eggs at one time. Before that happens, a female must mate with a male. There are various ways that millipede couples can get together. Some males court their mates by serenading them. They may rub their legs against their bodies the way crickets do or drum with their feet on the ground. Others produce perfumes for the females to smell or a sweet-tasting substance that a female can lick off the male's back. Still other male millipedes spin a silk thread that leads the female to the mating place.

After mating, the female lays her eggs in a hole in the ground or in rotting leaf matter. After a week or so, tiny millipedes hatch from the eggs. Some species have only six legs when they hatch; others have up to twenty. The little millipedes are white or purplish in color because their exoskeletons are very thin. The exoskeleton hardens and thickens with each molt, making the millipedes look darker. As the millipedes grow, they molt again and again. Each time, they add more body segments and more pairs of legs.

DID YOU KNOW?
Millipedes can climb up trees and even walk upside down. Their legs are specially adapted for gripping the surface as they move along.

MILLIPEDE PETS

The most common millipedes you're likely to find around your home are those little brown ones that are about an inch (2.5 cm) long. The best places to look for them are in leaf piles and rotting logs, under rocks, and down in the soil. Don't forget to bring a trowel to dig up the soil, a plastic spoon to scoop up the millipedes, and a collecting jar. Since millipedes don't move very fast, you won't have much trouble catching them.

Millipedes vs. Centipedes

When you're looking for millipedes, make sure you don't collect any centipedes by mistake. Many people often confuse millipedes and centipedes. Although these two are close relatives, they are very different creatures.

While millipedes may make good pets, centipedes do not. Here's what to look for:

Millipedes	Centipedes
Usually tube-shaped body	Usually flattened body
Two pairs of legs per segment	One pair of legs per segment
Two to three hundred legs	Usually less than a hundred legs
Short antennae	Long antennae
Move slowly in random directions	Move quickly in an "S" pattern
Scavengers and decomposers	Predators
Do not bite	Can bite and inject venom (poison) into victim

Finding millipedes around your home is easy enough, but you won't find any of those big ones that are almost a foot long, unless you live in a tropical area. Many pet stores sell these giant millipedes. They make very interesting pets, but they are difficult to care for and could be dangerous. Like their mini-relatives, giant millipedes do not bite or sting, but they can produce bad-smelling chemicals that can make you sick. They don't get used to being handled and may react defensively, squirting or oozing their chemicals at any time. These giant millipedes often carry mites, tiny parasites that not only make the millipedes ill, but can cause rashes or other allergic reactions in people.

INTERNET RESOURCES

www.earthfoot.org/backyard/1000legs.html "Centipedes, Millipedes & Pill Bugs"

www.ext.colostate.edu/pubs/insect/05552.html "Millipedes, Centipedes, and Sowbugs"

www.uky.edu/Agriculture/Entomology/entfacts/struct/ef645.htm "Millipedes"

www.okstate.edu/OSU_Ag/agedcm4h/pearl/insects/grdnbugs/f-7316.pdf "Centipedes and Millipedes"

FAST FACTS

Scientific name	*Mantis religiosa* (European mantis) in Family Mantidae (mantises)
Cost	Can be caught free around your home; an egg case costs about $10.
Food	Live insects, including crickets, grasshoppers, flies, and moths
Housing	A 5- or 10-gallon (19- or 38-liter) tank (with a mesh lid). Include a large, branched twig for the mantis to climb on. Lightly spray water into the container every few days and use a small sponge in a shallow container as a water source. The praying mantis may drink water from a spoon.
Training	Praying mantises do everything by instinct. They cannot be taught behaviors.
Special Notes	Praying mantises generally need to live in a warm environment of 75°F (24°C) or higher. If you buy a praying mantis egg case in the fall or winter, keep it in the refrigerator until springtime. Otherwise, the baby mantises will hatch in the middle of winter when it's too cold to go outside. Make sure it is okay to release the mantises in your area.

PRAYING MANTIS

HOW WOULD YOU LIKE a pet that looks like it came from another planet? The praying mantis has a triangular-shaped head, big, bulging eyes, and a long, green body that makes it look like one of those "little green men" from Mars. But this is no alien; it's an insect that lives right here on Earth.

The praying mantis is a hunter that preys mostly on other insects and eats them alive! If you keep one of these critters as a pet, you won't believe your eyes when you watch it gobble up its dinner.

HUNTER IN HIDING

The praying mantis may be a unique-looking creature, but it has typical insect parts: six legs, a three-part body, two antennae, and an exoskeleton. Its size may range from 2 to 6 inches (5 to 15 cm) long. The male is usually smaller than the female.

The praying mantis has two sets of wings. The top ones are narrow and leathery. Folded underneath are large fan-shaped wings. Although a praying mantis can fly, it prefers to stay grounded. Even when it does take flight, it usually doesn't go very far.

Praying mantises are very helpful in gardens because they eat various insect pests, such as flies, aphids, moths, caterpillars, and grasshoppers. But they also eat bees, butterflies, and even each other!

Many praying mantises are green or brown and blend into their surroundings. This camouflage helps them hide from both predators and prey. A hungry animal may not notice a green mantis sitting on a green leaf or a brown one against the bark of a tree. (Praying mantises that live in the tropics match the vivid colors of tropical flowers.)

Praying mantises spend a lot of time sitting perfectly still on trees or plant leaves, waiting in hiding for unsuspecting prey to come by. After spotting something interesting, such as a fluttering moth, the mantis tracks its movements. If necessary, it can turn its head to see things behind it without moving its body.

Compound Eyes

The two big bulging eyes that help make a praying mantis look so alien are compound eyes. Each one is made up of thousands of tiny lenses. Each lens focuses on one small part of the mantis's environment. The many tiny images seen through these lenses fit together to form a single large picture, much as the many colored tiles of a mosaic fit together to make a large picture. Compound eyes are very good for spotting moving objects—an important ability for a hunter. The mantis also has three small simple eyes, each with a single lens, between the compound eyes. They detect light and dark. The shadow of a predator warns the mantis to fly away.

When its prey is within reach, the praying mantis quickly leaps out of hiding and snatches the insect with its front legs. These legs have sharp spines that allow the mantis to catch and hold on to its prey. It uses its sharp jaws to munch on its prey while it's still alive and squirming. After finishing a meal, the praying mantis cleans itself thoroughly, running a leg all over its body and even inside its mouth, to remove stray bits of the insect.

DID YOU KNOW?

Many praying mantises have one ear on their thorax. It is specially tuned to listen for the ultrasounds of bats, which are the mantis's natural predator. If a mantis hears a bat, it will quickly dive to the ground or fly in the opposite direction.

MAKING MORE MANTISES

"Everybody knows" that a female praying mantis eats the male after they mate. But it isn't really true! This common myth is probably based on the fact that both of them are hungry after mating. Mantis breeders usually do not feed a mating couple, to keep from distracting them. Eating the mate does not occur very often in the wild. If it does, the male is as likely to eat the female as she is to eat him.

The real story is much less dramatic. When a female is ready to mate, she sends out a chemical that lures a male to her. The male spreads out his wings and curls his abdomen to get her attention. If the female likes what she sees, she will hold out her front legs to welcome him. The male climbs onto the female's back and they mate, staying together for as long as five hours.

A little over a week later, the female is ready to lay her eggs. Hanging upside down on a twig far above the ground, she releases soft, sticky foam from the end of her body. Then she moves in circles as she lays her fertilized eggs in the foam. The foam dries and hardens to form an egg case about the size of a walnut. The female may make several more egg cases before winter. Each one may contain up to 100 eggs.

Adult praying mantises do not live to see winter, but their offspring are safe and protected inside their cozy egg case. In the spring, tiny nymphs squeeze through slits at the bottom of the egg case. They look like miniature praying mantises, but they do not have wings yet. These newly hatched nymphs are already too big for their exoskeleton so they must molt. Once their new exoskeleton has hardened, they are starving. They search for small insects to eat and will even eat each other. The young mantises will molt six to nine times before they become adults with fully formed wings. By then it is late summer, and they will live for only a few months more.

PRAYING MANTIS PETS

The most common types of praying mantis found in North America are the European mantis, Chinese mantis, and the Carolina mantis. They live throughout the eastern United States. If you live in this part of the country, you can look for praying mantises in your own neighborhood. You may see one sitting on the side of a house, a windowsill, a car, or lawn furniture. It's not easy to find them, though, because they are so territorial—there may be only one mantis in an entire garden.

It's usually fairly easy to catch a praying mantis once you find one. Approach it slowly, then hold your hand out in front of it, and it will walk onto your hand. It will not bite you. Even if it strikes you with its spiny front legs, they are too delicate to break your skin.

If you can't find a praying mantis around your home, you can order an egg case from a biological supply company. Then you can watch lots of little mantises come into the world for the first time. After they are big enough to eat small crickets, keep only one or two and set the rest free outside. These insects do best when they are housed alone; otherwise, they may eat one another.

INTERNET RESOURCES

www.szdocent.org/ff/f-mantid.htm "Praying Mantids"

www.ex.ac.uk/bugclub/mantids.html "Praying Mantid Caresheet"

www.easyinsects.co.uk/mantis/ "Praying Mantis—How to Care for Praying Mantis"

FAST FACTS

Scientific name	*Helix aspersa* (common garden snail); *Achatina fulicia* (giant African land snail) in Class Gastropoda (snails and slugs) of Phylum Mollusca (mollusks)
Cost	Free: Common garden snails can be caught around your home.
Food	Fruits and vegetables, such as cucumbers, lettuce, apples, bananas, peaches, melons, and pears. Also need cuttlefish bone for calcium (found at the pet store).
Housing	A 5- or 10-gallon (19- or 38-liter) tank (with a mesh lid). Put 2 to 3 inches (5 to 8 cm) of soil in the bottom. Then add a layer of dead and fallen leaves. Provide a couple of large stones for the snails to hide under. Lightly spray water into the container every few days and keep a wet cotton ball or piece of paper towel on the bottom to keep things moist. Keep the snail home out of direct sunlight.
Training	Snails do everything by instinct. They cannot be taught behaviors.
Special Notes	It is illegal to own giant African land snails in many U.S. states and other countries. If these snails escape in non-native areas, they can cause a lot of damage. Check with your local wildlife agency.

SNAILS

A SNAIL IS FAMOUS for carrying its home on its back. Unlike a hermit crab, a snail is actually attached to its shell, and the shell grows along with the snail.

A snail is a cute little creature as it peeks out of its attractive spiral shell. Underneath this hard outer covering is the snail's soft, slimy body. It leaves a trail of slime wherever it goes. If you don't mind a little slime, then maybe you'd like to keep a snail pet.

A LIFE OF SLIME

Everybody knows that a snail moves really slowly. After all, it has only one "foot." It doesn't hop, though—it glides. A snail's foot is long and soft, and covered with sticky slime. This slime is mucus, produced by a gland in the foot. The sticky slime helps to keep the snail from drying out. It also helps the snail grip surfaces as it moves. So it can crawl up and over rocks, stick fast to the underside of a twig or leaf, or climb up a wall. You can see where a snail has been by looking for a trail of silvery sticky slime.

A snail's head is at the front end of its foot. Attached to the head are two sets of tentacles. One long pair are eyestalks, with a tiny eye at the tip of each one. A snail has very poor eyesight; its eyes can detect only light and dark. The shorter tentacles pick up odors or chemicals in the air, which let the snail know where to find food.

Snails are often found in gardens because that's where their favorite food is— tasty plant leaves. The snail literally rips the leaves apart. It has a long tongue, called a radula, which is covered with thousands of tiny, sharp teeth. As the snail eats, it moves its radula back and forth like a file, shredding the leaf, then takes up the shredded bits of food into its mouth. A group of hungry snails can do a lot of damage to a vegetable garden.

When it is warm and sunny, a snail likes to hide out in cool, moist places, such as under rocks and logs, leaf piles, or deep in the soil. It comes out of hiding when it is cool and damp, especially at night or after a rain shower. If the weather is too hot and

> **DID YOU KNOW?**
> A slug is basically a snail without a shell.

dry, a snail will protect its moist body by hiding inside its shell. It will seal off the shell opening with a thin layer of mucus. As the mucus becomes dry and hard, it forms a watertight plug that holds moisture inside. The snail's body systems slow down, just as if it were hibernating, and it does not eat. When the dry spell is over, the snail will break the seal and emerge from its shell.

When a snail is bothered or threatened, it will tuck its head into its shell. Despite this defense, lots of snails get eaten by predators. A snail's shell does not do a perfect job of protecting the snail's soft body. For example, a bird may pick up a snail with its beak and knock it against a rock until the shell cracks. Some animals, however, do not eat snails because they don't like the slimy taste.

A SLIMY RITUAL

Each snail has both male and female parts, but it still needs a partner to mate. Before mating can take place, the two snails take their time getting to know each other. They move slowly as they circle each other, leaving a thick trail of slime. As they do their little slime dance, they touch each other with their tentacles, rub their heads together and "kiss," and press the "soles" of their feet together.

At some point, each snail shoots out a small, sharp dart made of a shell-like substance into the other snail's body. Exactly why snails do this is not known, but scientists think that this "love dart" may be a way to let the other snail know it is a chosen mate. It may also help to get their bodies ready for the mating process.

After they finish mating, which can take several hours, the two snails go their separate ways. A week or two later, each one lays its eggs—from twenty to a hundred or more. Many snails dig a hole in the soil and lay their eggs there, while others may lay them under rocks, rotting leaves, or logs. When the eggs are ready to hatch, they crack and little snails emerge. They look like tiny versions of their parents. They even have their own little shells, but these shells are very thin and soft. A baby snail's first meal is its eggshell, which provides minerals for building up its coiled shell. As the snail grows, the shell grows too, and becomes harder and thicker.

SNAIL PETS

You won't have much trouble catching a snail, since it moves so slowly. But first, you have to find it. That could be a little tricky since snails often hide during the day. You can search all over your yard, in flower beds, vegetable gardens, under piles of leaves, logs, or stones. When you find one, be careful when you put it in your collecting jar. Tiny snail shells are fragile and may break when you pick them up. It would be better to use a small paintbrush and sweep the little snail into the jar.

Living on Land

Some snails spend their lives on land, while others live in ponds, rivers, or the sea. But millions of years ago all *snails lived in water. Some of them developed a lung for breathing air and came up to the surface to breathe. The snails that lived in ponds or in shallow parts of the ocean sometimes came out onto the nearby lands to look for food. Gradually, some of these snails adapted to a full-time life on land.*

Snails may be as tiny as a pinhead or as large as your fist. The giant African land snail is the largest of all land snails, with a shell that may grow as large as 8 inches (20 cm) long. But the snails you may see in your garden will probably have shells about an inch (2.5 cm) long.

Some people have races with their snail pets. You have to have a lot of patience to watch this kind of race. Use a stopwatch to time how long a snail race takes. Then you can really see how slowly these snails move. Record which one wins and try again.

INTERNET RESOURCES

www.kiddyhouse.com/Snails/snail.html "All About Snails"

www.geocities.com/heartland/valley/6210/index1.htm "Giant African Land Snails"

www.irms.freeserve.co.uk/landsnail.html "The Giant African Landsnail"

www.expage.com/petzone2 "Pet Zone: Snails"

freespace.virgin.net/simon.senn/snailpag.htm "Suzanne's Snail Page"

FAST FACTS

Scientific name	*Aphonopelma seemanni* (Costa Rican zebra); *Grammostola rosea* (Chilean rose hair); *Avicularia avicularia* (pink-toed tarantula); *Aphonopelma chalcodes* (Mexican blond tarantula) in Family Theraphosidae
Cost	$20 to $25 in a pet store
Food	Live food, may include crickets, moths, caterpillars. (Insects can be caught at home, but crickets can also be bought in a pet store.) Provide a small shallow dish of water for drinking.
Housing	A 5 or 10-gallon (19- or 38-liter) tank (with a mesh lid). Put 2 to 3 inches (5 to 8 cm) of soil in the bottom. Provide a turned-over, broken plant pot for the spider to hide under. Lightly spray water into the container every few days to keep things moist. Keep the environment at a warm temperature of at least 70° to 75°F (21° to 24°C).
Training	Frequent handling can make a tarantula "friendlier." But be careful—if it falls, its exoskeleton could crack open and it may die. Some species are very fast and may escape.
Special Notes	Do not release tarantula pets in a non-native area. Tarantulas cannot survive in cold climates. Return the animal to a pet shop or a breeder if you cannot keep it. Tarantulas will eat other tarantulas, so keep them each in a separate container.

TARANTULAS

TARANTULAS ARE THE LARGEST spiders in the world. Their big, hairy bodies make them look scary and dangerous. For centuries, people believed that tarantulas were deadly spiders. The truth is, they rarely bite people. And even if they do, the venom of most tarantulas is not very strong. No one has ever died from a tarantula bite. Actually, their bites are said to be no more harmful to people than a bee sting.

Although many people find these big, hairy spiders scary or "creepy," others say that tarantulas are fun and fascinating and make great pets. In fact, tarantulas have been popular pets for a number of years.

> ### The Spider Dance
>
> The name "tarantula" came from a superstition that dates back to the sixteenth century. At the time, people believed that wolf spiders, found around Taranto, Italy, caused a disease called tarantism in their victims. Supposedly, this illness could be cured by a lively dance, called the tarantella. When the Europeans settled in the New World, they found big, hairy spiders and called them tarantulas. But these New World tarantulas belong to a different family than the European wolf spiders.

TARANTULAS IN THE WILD

Tarantulas are found mainly in warm regions, such as the southern and western United States and throughout the tropics. There are more than 800 kinds of tarantulas. Some of them live on the ground, others live in trees, and still others live in burrows. These spiders are known for their large size. The average tarantula has a 2-inch (5-cm) body and a leg span of 4 to 5 inches (10 to 13 cm). Some of the largest tarantulas are found in the tropics. The Goliath tarantula of South America may have a 3.5-inch (9-cm) body and a leg span of 10 inches (25 cm). It has been known to eat lizards and frogs, and sometimes dead birds.

Some people think spiders are insects. But they aren't. Spiders belong to a different group of animals, called arachnids, which also include ticks, mites, and scorpions. Unlike an insect, which has three body parts, an arachnid's body is made up of *two* main parts: the cephalothorax (a combination of the head and upper body) and the abdomen. And spiders do not have wings or antennae. Also, insects have six legs, while spiders have eight.

A spider's eight many-jointed walking legs have tiny claws on the tips that help them hold onto surfaces as they climb up things like trees or walls. In addition, two small pedipalps with sticky pads on the tips are attached to the spider's mouth. A spider uses its pedipalps like a fork and spoon to hold onto its prey and bring it to its mouth. Between the pedipalps are clawlike jaws, called chelicerae. At the end of each chelicera are the spider's fangs. These are long, hollow teeth, which are connected to glands that make venom (poison). When a tarantula sinks its fangs into its prey, venom flows into the victim's body. Spiders use venom to make their prey weak and helpless or even kill it.

On top of a tarantula's head is a cluster of eight tiny eyes. Despite all these eyes, a tarantula cannot see very well. It relies more on touch, taste, and smell to let it know about its surroundings. It doesn't have a nose, but it can detect chemicals in the air with special sense organs on its feet. And it can "taste" the air with highly sensitive hairs on the legs and pedipalps.

Like all spiders, tarantulas have spinnerets, two fingerlike organs that shoot out a liquid that hardens into silk. But tarantulas don't spin webs to sit in as other spiders do. Instead, the silk may be used to line underground burrows, to make a bed of silk for a place to molt, to wrap their prey to keep it under control, and to wrap their eggs.

Tarantulas wait for their prey to come to them. These nighttime hunters may wait for four or five weeks for suitable prey, which may include insects such as crickets, grasshoppers, and moths, as well as small mice, birds, frogs, and other spiders. When one of these creatures comes close, the tarantula runs a few steps and grabs it with its chelicerae. It brings the prey to its fangs and injects venom into its body. Now the creature can no longer move, and the tarantula chomps on its body.

Tarantulas usually run and hide from larger predators. But if they are attacked, they use their body hairs as a weapon, much as a porcupine does with its quills. The tarantula's body is covered with very sensitive hairs, most heavily on the abdomen. When it is bothered or threatened, a tarantula will flick off hairs from its abdomen at its enemy. These hairs are covered with a chemical that irritates the animal's eyes and nasal passages. (Only the hairs on the abdomen are harmful.)

TARANTULA PETS

With so many kinds of tarantulas, which one would make a good pet? Some of the most popular ones include the Mexican blond, the Chile rose hair, the pink-toed tarantula, and the Costa Rican zebra. It is a good idea to research these tarantulas before you buy one.

Adult male tarantulas don't make very good pets. They don't live long after they reach adult size, soon after they have mated. But females can live for a very long time, usually fifteen to twenty years.

Tarantulas may become nervous when they are being handled. You need to be very gentle because they will flick their hairs if they are handled roughly. Then your skin may get red, swollen, and itchy. Always wash your hands after touching a tarantula. You may get their hairs into your eyes if you rub them, and this can cause some serious irritation. Frequent handling can help the tarantula get used to being held.

Tarantulas don't usually bite, but they may grab hold of your finger with their fangs if they are in danger of falling. Tarantula bites are generally not dangerous, but they may cause allergic reactions in some people. It is a good idea to wear protective gloves when handling a tarantula.

INTERNET RESOURCES

exoticpets.about.com/library/weekly/aa021300a.htm "Tarantulas as Pets"

www.ex.ac.uk/bugclub/tarant.html "Tarantula Caresheet"

www.pma.edmonton.ab.ca/natural/insects/projects/zebra.htm "The Provincial Museum of Alberta Natural History: Invertebrate Zoology—Fact Sheet—Zebra Tarantula"

www2.tltc.ttu.edu/thomas/classPet/1999/Tarantula/facts.htm "Tarantula Facts"

NOT A PET!

In 1966 an eight-year-old boy picked up three large snails with pretty shells while vacationing in Hawaii with his family. He put them in his pocket, and took them back home with him to North Miami. When his mother discovered the snails, she told the boy to get rid of them. He let them free in his backyard, where they thrived and multiplied in the warm Florida climate. By 1969, giant snails were eating up garden plants and scraping the paint off the fronts of Miami houses. Pest-control experts estimated that there were 20,000 of these giant African land snails in just a thirteen-square-block area! Poison baits didn't work, so state and federal agriculture workers launched campaigns to pick up all the snails by hand. Meanwhile, children carried pet snails on school buses and spread them to new neighborhoods. If the snails were to spread throughout Florida and neighboring states, they could cause millions of dollars of damage to crops each year. In 1972 the control efforts finally wiped out all the giant African snails. The federal government made importing these snails illegal, with penalties of a $5,000 fine or up to five years in prison!

An animal that could become a pest if it escapes or is released is not a good choice for a pet, no matter how interesting or attractive it may be. That goes not only for species that can cause million-dollar crop damage but also for animals that could cause problems in your own home. Escapes from an ant farm would not be much of a nuisance; a few stray ants would soon die out. But some other insects, such as common cockroaches, would not be a wise pet choice in *any* household. Cockroaches are actually rather interesting and not really "dirty" as most people believe, but if a few escaped, you would soon have a home full of cockroach *pests*. Cunning and quick, these creatures multiply rapidly, and can survive under the worst conditions. They also contaminate food and spread germs, and their droppings can give some people asthma attacks. (The Madagascar hissing cockroach does make a good pet, as long as you get only males.)

Animals that bite or sting can also cause problems. If you're not willing to wear gloves when handling them and to take other safety precautions, forget about keeping tarantulas and other poisonous pets.

Many of the animals described in this book are "cheap pets" and can even be picked up for free in your neighborhood or a nearby park, beach, or farm. They are plentiful enough that taking a few would not disturb the natural community. Most "creepy crawlies" are temporary pets, though. They are interesting to keep for a while, to watch how they live and grow. You can even observe things that you would not be able to see in nature—such as the interactions in an ant colony or the soil-enriching activities of earthworms and millipedes. Always treat them with respect. They may be "cheap," but they are living creatures and can feel pain, satisfaction, and other sensations. After you have enjoyed them for a while, let them go—if possible, in a place close to where you originally found them.

FOR FURTHER INFORMATION

Note: Before attempting to keep a kind of pet that is new to you, it is a good idea to read one or more pet manuals about that species or breed. Check your local library, pet shop, or bookstore. Search for information on the species or breed on the Internet.

BOOKS

Clarke, Dave. *Keeping Creepy Crawlies.* New York: Barron's Educational Series, 2000.

Cutler, Warren. *Creepy Crawly Creatures.* Washington, DC: National Geographic Society, 1996.

Kneidel, Sally. *Creepy Crawlies and the Scientific Method.* Golden, CO: Fulcrum Publishing, 1993.

———. *Pet Bugs.* New York: John Wiley and Sons, 1994.

———. *More Pet Bugs.* New York: John Wiley and Sons, 1999.

Landau, Elaine. *Minibeasts as Pets.* Danbury, CT: Children's Press, 1997.

Pipe, Jim. *The Giant Book of Bugs and Creepy Crawlies.* New York: Copper Beach Books, 1998.

Ross, Mandy. *Creepy Crawlies* (Usborne Hotshots Series). Newton, MA: ECD Publications, 1996.

INTERNET RESOURCES

projects.edtech.sandi.net/marvin/bugs/ "Creepy Crawlies" by Marilyn Henetz

teach.fhu.edu/technology/EDU330/creepy.htm "Creepy Crawlies"

wildlifeeducation.tripod.com/creepycrawlies.html "Creepy Crawlies"

www.bbc.co.uk/reallywild/features/cc_index.shtml "BBC—Nature—The Really Wild Zone—Features—Creepy Crawlies"

www.beritsbest.com/CreaturesGreatandSma/CreepyCrawlies/index.shtml "Berit's Best: Creepy Crawlies"

www.ent.iastate.edu "Insects on the Web—Iowa State University Entomology"

www.pbs.org/wnet/nature/alienempire/ "NATURE: Alien Empire"

www.pbs.org/wgbh/nova/odyssey/hotsciencehouse/ "NOVA Online: Odyssey of Life: House Creepy Crawlies"

www.stemnet.nf.ca/CITE/creepy_crawlies.htm "Gander Academy's Creepy Crawlie Resources on the Web"

INDEX

Page numbers in *italics* refer to illustrations.